A Beginning-to-Read Book

BIG FEELINGS

FEELING SHY

by Mary Lindeen

NORWOOD HOUSE PRESS

DEAR CAREGIVER, The *Beginning to Read* Big Feelings books support children's social and emotional learning (SEL). SEL has been proven to promote not only the development of self-awareness, responsibility, and positive relationships but also academic achievement.

Current research reveals that the part of the brain that manages emotion is directly connected to the part of the brain that is used in cognitive tasks such as problem solving, logic, reasoning, and critical thinking—all of which are at the heart of learning.

SEL is also directly linked to what are referred to as 21st Century Skills: collaboration, communication, creativity, and critical thinking. The books included in this SEL series offer an early start to help children build the competencies they need for success in school and life.

In each of these books, young children will learn how to recognize, name, and manage their own feelings while learning that everyone shares the same emotions. This helps them develop social competencies that will benefit them in their relationships with others, which in turn contributes to their success in school. As they read, children will also practice early reading skills by reading sight words and content vocabulary.

The reinforcements in the back of each book will help you determine how well your child understands the concepts in the book, provide different ideas for your child to practice fluency, and suggest books and websites for additional reading.

The most important part of the reading experience with these books—and all others—is for your child to have fun and enjoy reading and learning!

Sincerely,

Mary Lindeen

Mary Lindeen, Author

Norwood House Press

For more information about Norwood House Press please visit our website at www.norwoodhousepress.com or call 866-565-2900.
© 2022 Norwood House Press. Beginning-to-Read™ is a trademark of Norwood House Press.
All rights reserved. No part of this book may be reproduced or utilized in any form or
by any means without written permission from the publisher.

Editor: Judy Kentor Schmauss   **Designer**: Sara Radka

Photo Credits: Getty Images: Antonio_Diaz, 26, charlie schuck, 18, Elva Etienne, 6, eyecrave, 21, Fly View Productions, 22, Hill Street Studios, 9, Imageegaml, 14, Imagesbybarbara, 17, JGalione, 10, JGI/Jamie Grill, 5, Johner Images, 25, Kinzie+Riehm, 29, Mark van Dam, 13, SDI Productions, 3; Shutterstock: Evgenyrychko, cover, Evgenyrychko

Library of Congress Cataloging-in-Publication Data has been filed and is available at catalog.loc.gov

Library ISBN: 978-1-68450-816-7   Paperback ISBN: 978-1-68404-672-0

PO339N—082021
Manufactured in the United States of America in North Mankato, Minnesota.

Have you ever felt a little scared
when meeting someone new?

Do you feel like you want
to hide or just disappear?

Everyone feels that way sometimes.

It's okay.

You might just be feeling shy.

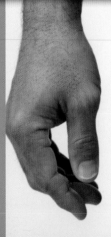

How do you know if you are feeling shy?

You might just want to watch everyone else for a few minutes.

You might want to stand or sit quietly next to someone you know.

It can take a little time to decide how you feel about someone new.

How can you tell if someone else is feeling shy?

They might be standing apart from everyone else.

They might be holding the hand of someone they trust, like a parent or a teacher.

They might be hiding their face.

They might not be
talking much—
or at all.

A person who is feeling shy just needs a little more time to feel comfortable.

Be patient.

Let them know
you are a friend
who will wait until
they are ready.

Sometimes it can help to just sit quietly next to someone who is feeling shy.

That helps them know they are not alone.

Show them
that you are a
nice person and
not scary.

You might even
make a new friend!

. . . READING REINFORCEMENT. . .

CONNECTING CONCEPTS

CLOSE READING OF NONFICTION TEXT

Close reading helps children comprehend text. It includes reading a text, discussing it with others, and answering questions about it. Use these questions to discuss this book with your child:

1. What does it mean to feel shy?

2. Do you think grown-ups ever feel shy? Why do you think so?

Once you have discussed the above questions, ask your child to either draw a picture of someone who is feeling shy or choose one of the children pictured on pages 3 to 11. Then ask the following questions about the child in the drawing or the photo:

1. How can you tell this person might be feeling shy?

2. What might be one reason this person is feeling shy?

3. How would you feel in that situation?

4. Do you ever feel shy? When?

5. When you feel shy, what do you do? How could someone else help you when you're feeling shy?

VOCABULARY AND LANGUAGE SKILLS

As you read the book with your child, make sure he or she understands the vocabulary used. Point to key words and talk about what they mean. Encourage children to sound out new words or to read the familiar words around an unfamiliar word for help reading new words.

FLUENCY

Help your child practice fluency by using one or more of the following activities:

1. Reread the book to your child at least two times while he or she uses a finger to track each word as it is read.

2. Read a line of the book, then reread it as your child reads along with you.

3. Ask your child to go back through the book and read the words he or she knows.

4. Have your child practice reading the book several times to improve accuracy, rate, and expression.

FURTHER READING FOR KIDS

Anderson, Shannon. *Too Shy to Say Hi*. Washington, DC: Magination Press, 2021.

Barnham, Kay. *Feeling Shy!* Minneapolis, MN: Free Spirit Press, 2017.

Freeland, Claire A. B. *What to Do When You Feel Too Shy: A Kid's Guide to Overcoming Social Anxiety*. Washington, DC: Magination Press, 2016.

FURTHER READING FOR TEACHERS/CAREGIVERS

Better Health Channel: Children and Shyness
https://www.betterhealth.vic.gov.au/health/HealthyLiving/shyness-and-children

Children's Hospital Los Angeles: Help Your Child Overcome Shyness
https://www.chla.org/blog/rn-remedies/help-your-child-overcome-shyness

Grow, by WebMD: Tips to Parent Your Shy Child
https://www.webmd.com/parenting/features/parent-shy-child#1

Feeling Shy uses the 89 words listed below. *High-frequency* words are those words that are used most often in the English language. They are sometimes referred to as sight words because children need to learn to recognize them automatically when they read. *Content* words are any words specific to a particular topic. Regular practice reading these words will enhance your child's ability to read with greater fluency and comprehension.

HIGH-FREQUENCY WORDS

a	have	much	they
about	help(s)	new	time
all	how	next	to
and	if	not	until
are	is	of	want
at	it	or	way
be	just	show	when
can	know	take	who
do	like	tell	will
even	little	that	you
few	make	the	
for	might	their	
from	more	them	

CONTENT WORDS

alone	felt	needs	shy
apart	friend	nice	sit
comfortable	hand	okay	someone
decide	hide	parent	sometimes
disappear	hiding	patient	stand(ing)
else	holding	person	talking
ever	it's	quietly	teacher
everyone	let	ready	trust
face	meeting	scared	wait
feel(ing, s)	minutes	scary	watch

About the Author

Mary Lindeen is a writer, editor, parent, and former elementary school teacher. She has written more than 100 books for children and edited many more. She specializes in early literacy instruction and books for young readers, especially nonfiction.